KEEPING STILL, MOUNTAIN

Also in this 1983 Ha'Penny Book Series:
    Jonathan Penner, *The Intelligent Traveler's
    Guide to Chiribosco*
    L.W. Michaelson, *On My Being Dead and Other Stories*

KEEPING STILL, MOUNTAIN

Poems by John Engman

Published by The Galileo Press, Baltimore 1983

Grateful acknowledgment is made to the editors of the publications in which the following poems first appeared:

The Antioch Review: "Alcatraz"; "One Way of Looking at Wallace Stevens"; "About the Deliverance of Men and Women from a Few Dark Buildings Overlooking Lowry Hill". *Crazyhorse:* "Einar"; "What Happened at the Funeral of *Life Magazine*"; "The Vital Statistic"; "Epigraph to be Repeated in a Steambath"; "One Minute of Night Sky". *The Iowa Review:* "The Absence of the Cabbage Moth"; "Poem with Sedative Effect". *Ironwood:* "Living in the Real World: Red Sunrise"; "Wishing". *Poetry Northwest:* "Sandcastles"; "From an Apartment on the Third Floor"; "Photogravure of a Winter with Oranges: Confessions for Paul and Vanessa". *The Missouri Review:* "Keeping Still, Mountain". *The Seattle Review:* "Photograph from an Old Album". *Sonora Review:* "How to Write Poetry with Your Clothes On"; "Meditation for the Sad Expression of the Grillwork Smile on Minnehaha Bus"; "Atlantis"; "In Winter"; "Poem with Nothing to Say". *Telescope:* "Transparent Highway Curves"; "Asteroids"; "Mushroom Clouds".

"Still Life 1961"; "The Dolphins" and "Rainer Maria Rilke Returns from the Dead to Address the Junior Military School at Sankt Pölten" first appeared with other poems in a limited-edition volume, *Alcatraz*, published by Burning Deck Press, 1980. "Rainer Maria Rilke Returns from the Dead to Address the Junior Military School at Sankt Pölten" was reprinted in *A Century in Two Decades*, A Burning Deck Anthology, Burning Deck Press.

Special thanks to the Minnesota State Arts Board for providing a grant in 1977, during which time some of these poems were written.

Cover art by Gyanesh
Cover Design by Jill Francis

For my mother and father

and I seem intimate with what I merely touch
— Frank O'Hara, "Poem"

CONTENTS:

*

*   *   *   *

Alcatraz

I can't recall the name of the old cafe
but I saw the famous San Francisco dream there
and people sipping chocolate while gazing at a blue bay.
A local woman made advances with a few remarks
about the deep, subconscious sea. I watched the gulls
circle tables, then I told them to go away.

I tried to put down on paper what made me
feel a certain way. I said rain was long black hair
in oceanic waves. But the sun was shining, as I remember,
and a blonde woman at the next table was memorable.
We talked until we found we held something in common,
both of us were Minnesotans and so we laughed until

we screamed. For a dime in the Automatic-Eye
I saw all I really cared to see of Alcatraz:
a man with a spyglass looking back at me. Gulls flew
across his polyester shirt, I could see him that clearly.
He must have watched me drinking my *cafe au lait!*
I saluted him across the bay. He raised an eyebrow.
Then a fatter woman ran at him with an Instamatic. *Edna!*
he must have said, *Come quick! People are waving.*

One Way of Looking at Wallace Stevens

How many steps would I have to take,
beginning from the day of my birth, to remain forever
in the same spot in space by compensating
for the slow rotation of the earth? Let me tell you about

the deep neglect of the universe: it hurts.
After I learned how the moon pulls at us, and further,
how the earth orbits a sun which follows a course that
drags us into darkness, never to return... it seems ridiculous.

Once I was a boy of seventeen.
I combed my greasy hair into oceanic ducks. There was
this girl, she had other limitations but she giggled at my jokes.
Her black dress, cut very low, her *aspic nipples* and... oh my soul.
She was seventeen like me but somehow old. When I saw her

through the straw of my coke
I felt naked like a fetus looking back
down into the future through the barrel of a photoscope.
Now *I* am old: not in the way of a woman, but like the scene
outside my window, a few blackbirds remaining in this world
like immigrants from books.

Thirteen blackbirds hopping on the same pale branch!
I sit by myself, on the wooden chair, like this: Buddha
with a sense of space and a bunch of blackbirds for my audience.
This tree supports my great distrust for all schools of thought.
I stand up, about to walk, as best I can: the tree erupts
like someone who has fallen half-asleep and seen the color red!

Or simply: blackbirds fly
like blackbirds startled by the sudden movement of a clumsy man.

Transparent Highway Curves

   My father never danced,
as he knew he should have, but gave his life
to the slow dissolve of an old Chevrolet sedan
he pushed up every steep street in Minneapolis,
an otherwise bombproof town. There was a war on
but he never wanted to fight or make anyone mad,
wasn't saving gas for a war effort, he was just
halfway home

   when a piston rammed
through the cylinder wall and another long road
stopped coming forward. My father drove all year,
lost Monday through Friday on the open road
and came home Saturday while the Chevrolet
sent up omens, huge sighs and puffs of smoke.
My father sold pencils and transparent highway
curves in the Black Hills

   and badlands of Dakota,
special instruments and blueprints showing
where the roads should go. My father never wanted
to be gay at the Moulin Rouge or sad at the Ritz
but he did want to conscientiously object
about what he thought was wrong with this world,
wanted his opinions heard by the only audience
he thought would listen: northern, walleye, bass.

But his sparkplugs got wet.
The engine failed. A last bald tire went flat.
My father said he saw a metaphor in all this,
but he couldn't remember what "metaphor" meant.
My father understood cars and fish but not much
about metaphor, nuclear warheads etc. He said
there was nothing much wrong with this world
he could change

but himself. So when the Chevy stalled
he didn't just get philosophical, he walked.
Pulling fish from Lake Mille Lacs was his only
demonstration of force: northern, walleye, bass.
He sat there in a rowboat, going nowhere, all talk.
This world, he said, I can't do anything about it.
He apologized, his voice rising from the water
into thin air, *I can't do anything about it*
echoing, changing planets.

Living in the Real World: Red Sunrise

My father believed in Alaska, sitting around
Minnesota he followed The Great Highway with his thumb.
The Great Highway was a series of tiny red dots on a map
he had purchased from the Esso at 66th. He ran his thumb

around the borders of Alaska
gingerly, the way a cruder man might have explored
curves and shadows rented in the rooms of a Klondike brothel.
Someplace far away was what he wanted, set in a snowy valley,

and with bricks of gold piled by the highway
and abandoned because of the high value men placed
on landscapes littered with the fallen bones of heaven.
One of the most tiring things in human history —

Minneapolis in the fifties. 1961,
in the crater of a moviehouse, my father felt a sharp
chest pain at the end of the movie *South Pacific.*
Paradise had stopped his heart.

It could not compare with his own stark version
of Alaska, one room of a suburban bungalow in Minneapolis
inhabited by rare creatures: cannonball headboard, hutch mirror,
triple dresser. Sunlight streaks on a threadbare carpet were

arrows pointing the way down an imaginary road
and out the window, out into the winter and the natural world
surfacing in red like an emotion that has been repressed: sitting
around in Minnesota, watching snow fall, watching the road grow
   narrow.

The Absence of the Cabbage Moth

I was invisible at age 12,
severe and devoted to questions

about plant and animal kingdoms.
I asked, nobody answered back,

I felt invisible because of this.
Anything I was willing to ask

was an act: willing my becoming
visible, simply *willing.* I walked

downstairs into illusions mother
kept her silence about: how and what

death of the red cat, who and why
and what gave the life to a white crocus.

If the perfect corpse of wax apples,
pears and melons in a wooden bowl

couldn't hold her attention, who was
I? I asked if this illusion meant

an imperfection in the world was false.
She wouldn't say. It was her silence

that affected me like alcohol.
Somehow I expressed myelf: big white

soft shirt, rose gabardines, a hurt look.
I asked, kept asking: *Who are we now?*

Is this condition permanent? Is
uncertainty like garden darkness

only a mirror to be pushed and
pushed away without success? What good

news makes sense as it enters the world?
What next? Is death or rain predicted

by the absence of the cabbage moth?
Mother, please describe the cabbage moth

the red cat and white crocus in great
detail, tell me all about myself.

Still Life 1961

Father balanced with his tripod on a rock,
judged us, judged the sun
and then he squeezed us very hard
but carefully, into the Kodak.
This is how the camera works I thought,
somehow making people small,
like the mind it plays tricks. "How
do we get out of there?" I asked
but nobody laughed, nobody felt
it made much difference:
mother served her rhubarb,
gramps looked away,
sister went on jabbering
about her dance at the bazaar.
Such display annoyed me.
It was a lovely afternoon,
how could I cut a realistic figure
buckled-up, dwarfed
and bathed by summer light
but all the best of me
eaten by photographic acids?
It was a lovely afternoon,
the shutter clicked,
or was it mother who clicked
her tongue because my skin
was chalk and hair mussed?
Sister cut my silhouette from crepe.
I complained because no boy
could be so tattered at the edge.
I said I thought the light was wrong
and it was darkness silhouettes know most about.
Father tried to visualize

three generations in the sun,
but the light *was* wrong. The shutter clicked.
Father said he saw me inside the black box
(this memory because the mind plays tricks)
and looking in I saw myself reversed
in the ground glass, disfigured,
looking back: my eyes were hazel brown
but almond-shaped and dimly lit, adult.

Photograph From an Old Album

Picture, if you will, the 90 per cent
   of the universe
that has disappeared. It seemed like home:
   galaxies swallowed by black holes
and creatures of intelligence
and orbs and spheres
removed from the museum of the here and now.
   Remember the emotion
of assorted men
and women who just wandered off
amid the peonies in sorry-looking outfits
on the earth a century ago.

In vaudeville comics pulled off stage
by hooks left shadowy curtains
for the audience to watch. Now look:
   in a room with curtains drawn apart
the here and now is another curtain
drawn between the real world and your window.
It is a fluid swirling around the embryo,
   or in the photograph from an old album
   forms a curtain like your family:
blurred faces, slapped backs,
fans and big cigars
upstage the child in the weathered pram
   who has vanished
in the following photograph, or who appears
to be the boy with time on his hands
who rears back laughing at the clapboard house.

Wishing

for George

Here we are parked in the photograph of a Pontiac
with wheels made of snow. The snow has stopped
against the wheels like a flight of dead moths.
This is our winter migration, we have to walk.
You are in red, I in my old blue winter coat.
This is another storm in Minnesota, 1964.
We are going nowhere dressed so warm.
We are lost, as children tend to be, near home.

While we sat on the hood of this old sedan
our fathers shoveled and spoke about the end
a certain mystery could come to if we touched it
gently with our hands. This mystery
escaped the 8×5. It was the hammer of shovels
on hubcaps and the frozen road, our fathers'
breathing like a sound we'd never heard before
from nails driven into hard, wet wood.

As always the mystery is ruined by a photograph.
Photography is silence. Everyone knows that.
Photography is what we do to wish for too much.
Wishing is what our fathers did. We wish
we'd saved the photographs that show how
evolution fills the gaps: Pontiacs, our fathers
on the brink of happiness. Minnesota, 1964. Another
storm. We disappeared although we only meant to blink.

Einar

Wave after wave arrives. We are sitting in the sun
on Coney Island, 1955. The sea looks strong to us,
it has been trying to move forward for a very long time.
Einar sits in the wicker chair: cane, straw hat.
We have been trying to understand what the screamers
are screaming a mile or so away in the amusement park,
tourists plunging down toward earth on the Coney Island
Parachute. Silk parachutes retard their speed. The polka-dot

umbrellas on the boardwalk retard the sunlight and the sea-
breeze. The breeze howls toward Brooklyn, howls
like a ballad sung by someone big in an empty bathhouse.
Down the beach a child with a shovel from the five & dime
tunnels for China. We'll never see him again! Einar smiles.
We are burning up. Tipping a lemonade I've destroyed his straw hat.
But we don't mind because the sun is hot in the year of
Our Lord, 1955. This is Coney Island. Wave after wave arrives.

The Dolphins

In Florida, at the Aquatorium, dolphins
and my mother who had spoken with them in her native tongue,
Norwegian, nodded back and forth without understanding.
The man who made the dolphins jump with whips, blubber chunks
and smaller fish

    sat on the deck with his logbook
balancing cost versus credit for the waterwalk and somersault
through flaming hoops. Father was off somewhere, admiring big ideas
glassy sea and miles and miles of white beach put into his head.
I was naked in Key West,

    sunning in the buff,
eyeing girls as smooth as those I'd seen on travel posters.
Florida, my father said, was how he felt at first communion:
moonlit palms and bougainvillea coming on as holy spirits, bathers
in clogs and terrycloth, angels puffing up the hill to our motel.

    "Everything is what they said it was,"
my mother said, on postcards. A dolphin on her postcards
flew from the Aquatorium into summer air as a trainer
bared his whipping arm, the way a novice floating too far down
is suddenly raised by his instructor, pulled by the hair.

    We spent two weeks by the sea. Spent,
my father said, his whole payraise. We bought shells as souvenirs
and, it is impossible to say what we were thinking, saved
snapshots of the family escaping through a small Atlantic
painted on a huge screen. For 50¢ we could be anything:

Cuban dictators, divers, fishwives.
Pushing our heads through cutouts, posing as though in guillotines,
we became three dolphins who created monumental waves
on the mirrored sea. You can almost hear glass breaking.
Everything is what they said it was and we look free.

*   *   *   *

Asteroids

I belong here. Between the woman with the giant ass
and the shattered man who won't talk, between White
Russian and Manhattan, pompadour and beehive of blue hair.
I am the local stranger who grows stranger by the hour,
another body barmaids circle as if searching for a face
full of sensation, carrying the empties away.

All around me the cliches consume the atmosphere
and I listen carefully as if any country-western tune
may contain the lovesick line I need to reheat an icy barmaid.
But the barmaids know me, know what I'll say before I've begun,
my best joke: "There is no such thing as a bad check,
only a troubled one." The little men with rayguns
who steal my spare change

ravage earth from blazing videos
where I make my stand like a vagrant gazing into a flaming
Sterno can. The video window is so small only one emotion
can escape from a face on earth. I try to be brave.
What has become of my life is invisible after a few deathrays
and a few beers chased by a bump of something strong.
Nothing can suddenly go wrong—all barflies safe to devour
Happy Hour chicken-wings and grow old, more aliens
and nobodies than history can hold.

Sandcastles

In college my professor said the *abyss*
was no larger than a silver spot
that measures the collapse of one second
on a man's wristwatch. "This is a concept

adults must learn to live with."
When I showed him the nudes on my French postcards
he said it wasn't Art, he saw fallen breasts
as big tears on the face of a Grandfather Clock

and everybody laughed at sympathy he saw
between "the delicate curves of the prostate"
and what high seas had done to Edward Weston's
chambered nautilus. "Art," he said,

"means nothing feels safe as itself."
The girls at our college didn't feel safe with *him*.
He smelled of toilet soap from Woolworth's
and in student conferences he touched their knees.

The spring he was dismissed
he ran off with a freshman, Janice,
who had slept with everyone on campus
but him. "Janice is my anima," he said,

"I told my wife I needed
space and distance, a short-term relationship
is no disgrace, and she doesn't blame me. After all,
this is the 20th century. Janice says the same."

That summer, after Janice
entered therapy and his wife divorced him,
I received a letter postmarked California:

"I'm afraid someday I'll see myself in my children."

That was the last I heard from him.
His theory that in Art and life a man needed
"vision" was an artless and short-lived theory
professors of subsequent courses said to forget.

Now they encourage the human senses:
I can still smell his toilet soap from Woolworth's
and feel his weight move across the classroom,
I can hear him preach *Imagination, Reverie* and *Pain,*

and see him, by the chalkboard
swinging his pointer from concept to concept,
as if he was the last adult who stood and knocked
sandcastles into the Pacific with his white cane.

How to Write Poetry With Your Clothes On

The guy in the white T-shirt who represents despair
by sitting in a window of the diner in this poem
has had it up to here with unskilled labor.
The gal in the black apron generates malaise
but wants to generate something more, a new career.
T-shirt slurps coffee, apron chews gum —
the climax invented for this poem may never come —
nothing they feel feels dramatic enough,
nothing makes them laugh and cry.
My characters have gone on strike.

The diner is closed.
All the heartache this poem meant to convey
has been cancelled until further notice, diminished
by false impressions real life creates, called facts.
I have lost control of my own poem:
soon the sedan will demand the coupé,
platinum dream of the strawberry blonde,
accusations against the author will be
written in lipstick on paper napkins:

"You have such dumb ideas.
We want to live miles from the natural law,
no BBQ beef and chicken à la king, no free refills.
We don't want to wait on a ventriloquist
with soup du jour of your emotional left-overs.
We want desire to consume us, not diner flies.
We don't want to be identical, secondhand. Tell
the truth, that we are citizens of the Milky Way
and we can sing. We can make love. We can dance."

About the Deliverance of Men and Women From a Few Dark Buildings Overlooking Lowry Hill

Looking from my window, six a.m., I see somebody
in gym-shorts wave a tennis racket like the single wing
he believes will lift him into the cold dawn.
During the winter of '69, a similar scene: snow falls,

the mercury hits thirty-degrees-below-zero windchill and
I see her in a green Salvation Army parka that must weigh
thousands of pounds. She stamps, curses, waves her arms
as if she wants to soar into the wild blue yonder.

Down here on earth, in these dark buildings,
we seem to exist in an aurora of *I want, I want.*
As in everything on earth the exact meaning is often missed:

Dawgone, tuh thank us Earthfolk cud be sech idjuts!
Someday we should learn to live together in the perpetual moment:
one small step taken by the body toward the body of someone else.

From an Apartment on the Third Floor

Listening to voices in the hall
I hear A tell B that D has been sleeping
with E, F and G. Thud. B faints? Whack.
A strikes B? Silence. C? Perhaps I am C?
Later, watching from the transom, I see
the hallway ends like a poem, running
into a blank wall.

For a long time I support
my body-tonnage on a tipsy wooden chair,
maintaining equilibrium with all my muscles
and my brain. When I am sure I am alone
I go into the hall and watch the elevator
numbers glow back and forth until the doors
open: no one.

How much noise will a stone cause
falling from a prehistoric mountain? I love
the idea, falling before anyone was born,
such shyness. Such an idea makes me feel
unbalanced like Raskolnikov, spellbound
by the mad chrysanthemums held hostage
on his papered walls. Silence. *The stone*

falls. Perhaps the stone
is an unheard syllable uttered by a prehistoric
god for no one in the gardens of Raskolnikov?
Or perhaps, listening for voices, Raskolnikov
hears them without stone, without cause. I watch
the elevator numbers flash and glow until I see
a shooting star, a falling stone. Something
that seems to say "I love you all, so far."

Photogravure of a Winter With Oranges:
Confessions for Paul and Vanessa

The couple in the next apartment are making love
sound painful. I can just imagine
what must be quite obvious to them, the juice
of every vital organ boiling and becoming morning.
Let us call them Paul and Vanessa.
Paul will be snow in the morning,
he will have no special meaning in the afternoon.
Vanessa will be shame where snow would have done,
by evening a geyser of acid and sugar
as she sends her thumbnail on a secret mission
beneath the skin of an orange.

Snow and oranges represent their personal defects,
things that are harmless until put to use.
Paul is showing for the first time
his tendency to run amuck. Vanessa
exhibits her faithful breasts to the four walls.
Just think of the flare of his & her nostrils!
How very soon Paul will be found beautiful
by someone who has gone away (Vanessa
will be on a train headed into tomorrow
as if it exists, the room Paul is in will seem
crowded by a gentle breeze).

Let us say
endless meadows tiptoe through Vanessa,
bigger meadows clomp through Paul
and both of them are filled with miserable savannas
where the trees deposit oranges in the miserable snow.
Blizzards and squalls, Cleopatra and Rough Lemon.
This is the orchard in the photogravure I imagine

on the bureau behind them. Let us think
of Paul and his Vanessa as two strangers who have met
beneath a plate of glass, intaglio. Paul and Vanessa shot
with some fears in a picture.
I could never see them as real people
in a winter room.
In the foreground the oranges undone by the cold

are blacker than buckshot. Paul and Vanessa
are just
thunderclaps floating absentmindedly
among the trees. Paul is about to say something
utterly stupid. It is the nature of photography
that stops him. Everything seems about to begin
and end as a scream.
Maybe what it comes to is a man like me, making love
from oranges for Paul and Vanessa, making love from snow
that falls and as fast as it can turns perfectly black.

Epigraph to be Repeated in a Steambath

Tonight I want to set the world on fire.
It has been a long day of venom and sludge
and my mind is ablaze:
stalling the onrush of my sunset years
I invent a cocktail meant to cure dismay,
tequila cut with milk of magnesia, a Pepto-Dismal.
I am never strong enough to bless or kill
but the shot-glasses I ignite flare suddenly
like new disciples. Walls sway and burning
sensations come and go like seance
ghosts. Forbidden emotions
I keep alive in some male underzone
build heavens and send me an angel named
Little Richard, radio blaring
his ode to joy.

Fifty years from now I'll be a snoozer
in woolen slippers. In whirlpools
I'll sing the old Little Richard tune
about Miss Molly at the house of blue light.
Deaf and flimsy, I'll give my grandchildren
nightmares. They'll feed me prunes and shy away
as if I am a zoo animal. Mornings I don't die
I'll holler come rub the cold from my bones,
bring more Pepto-Dismals,
bring more pills and balms, more everything.
I will exude helplessness and see fireballs in the dayroom,
make eyes with *Playboy* centerfolds,
read prophecies of doom in oatmeal
and without effort become wise.

Mushroom Clouds

During the final minutes of the raid
Miss Nurvak made us kneel with our heads buried
between our knees—the blast that ruined our lives
was her yardstick breaking in half and confetti
she shredded over us was fallout. One boy threw up
Cheerios beneath his desk and then ran from class
with wet pants. The rest of us survived the drill
for milk and cookies during Miss Nurvak's nightmare
sermon on the Red Menace.

Miss Nurvak,
who said we have nothing to fear but fear itself,
was scared half-to-death. The shelter beneath her garden
was stocked with canned goods and sterilized water,
rations against the coming days of radioactive ash.
In gas mask and green fatigues, Miss Nurvak
would needlepoint and listen to the gramophone
until the fatal firestorms passed and she raised
her periscope, searching for pupils
from the lost second-grade.

So life was more serious than I thought.
And it was Miss Nurvak who made me want to be a man
as hard and strong as the stone man on the stallion
in the park, the general with epaulets of pigeon shit.
I imagined myself in crash helmet and bulletproof vest,
Miss Nurvak's periscope rising from the blackened grass:
how happy she would be to see a successful graduate
of Central Elementary who had not been reduced to ash
and whose ideals had not been shaken by the atomic blast
and who pushed the culprit forward with his bayonet,
a boy with wet pants.

What Happened at the Funeral of *Life Magazine*

Walter Cronkite watched me drink my beer.
It could have been any vintage fifties bar:
Julius Larosa sang on 45s to customers
with names like *Harry* for the men and *Edna* for the women.
I was called *chameleon* by the regular-johns
because I swiveled on my barstool from brunette to blonde.

It was almost an unpatriotic act:
I was young and strong, civilian. Everyone at the 2½
was a veteran of something: *Harry* of service in Korea,
Edna of marriage to *Harry.* When the President announced
the bombing of Cambodia, they awarded me another *Pabst Blue
    Ribbon.*

Johnson,
the guy who stacked glass, dumped garbage, mopped the bar
was blown to bits, sewn together, shipped home from Saigon
as a sponge-like mass, drugged and wired, kept alive by green
and yellow fluids pumped through coils into strictures. A portion

of his loin and flank had been replaced by plexiglass.
Sometimes, out of nowhere, Johnson shouted *Rat-a-tat-tat* . . .
and blew me off my barstool with a volley of bullets
from the handle of his mop. Down the bar the locals played
craps: juggle dice, slam the bar, count the black spots.

Rainer Maria Rilke Returns From the Dead to Address the Junior Military School at Sankt Pölten

Boys, these aches and pains will make us men.
It all depends on how you hurt yourself. Once,
I read about a boy my age, in *Time,* who became rain
by stepping on stones that explode beneath human weight.
Defying gravity, he rained from earth into the air and then
he rained more naturally as red and yellow ashes from the trees.
Boys, it all depends on how you hurt yourself. We will be shot.
In uniform. Again and again. In France or Spain. But in uniform
boys are men: when I was small my mother dressed me in a bonnet
and yellow frock. And I admit my admiration for the muscles of Rodin.
Sometimes love has been mistaken for the way we use our hands
but don't let them call you women. Let bedsprings scream: *Enough!*
I am a man. I saw Prague divided by a falling leaf.
And from a clinic window at Valmont I saw red and yellow leaves
falling and being blown away—that taught me all I want to know
about delayed allegiances. What makes us men will kill us all.
We stay alive by dreaming of the boys we used to be, who'd never
recognize us now: priests and aviators dressed in black or gray,
who don't know what to make of what, who tremble and obey.

Meditation for the Sad Expression
of the Grillwork Smile on Minnehaha Bus

One cold six-pack
and my early warning system grows numb. The empties
crowd the flattened grass like a miniature stonehenge.
Mushroom clouds roll around inside my skull and all
the prayers spoken centuries before I was born clatter
like bottlecaps in paper sacks or the wreckage of old
satellites still flying and forgotten in space.

The big-bang theory suggests this universe
will fall apart like pages blown from a scrapbook.
Eternity exists to give new meaning to the word *etcetera*.
But nothing ever happens here which can't be summarized
by an inch of newsprint, which can't be contained
by mace and billyclubs, which can't be praised
and forgotten on makeshift shrines. *The assassin*
pulls the trigger like a wishbone. The corpse sits up.

Bulldozers graze here like dinosaurs
and the yellow crane by the pond is a long mechanical arm
and large claw. Real swans stay as far as possible
from the shore of the city's highest crime area. One real
boy who has smoked too much marijuana has become clairvoyant
and charges into a future of darker and darker afternoons,
waving a switchblade. Everyday people are murdered here
but the universe is only wounded, swans circle slowly
and bums drink fast, dark lords of Minnehaha: searching
for the best mirage, waiting for the horsemen.

*   *   *   *

Atlantis

Everything that has been said for several centuries
is swept away by many hands and hurled through high windows
into a big hole my father calls *heaven* but I call *the sky*.
He looks angrily at me because I swore the human soul
was smaller and forlorn as any unmarked 8 oz. tin you pay
half-price for at the Railroad Salvage Grocery Store.

That was the night I thought he'd never learn
and I made foolish jokes about the boulevard in Minneapolis
where we both sat in darkness, watching yards where shadows
crawled between the bungalows like creatures from another world
and all the mothers who would never learn had hung loads
of white shirts and nighties like ghosts who are waiting

for Christ to return. I was 21 years old.
Already I had said too much: an immigrant from Norway, Michigan,
my father often spoke about another Norway where the sun
rose once but never set. *This world couldn't be your first,*
he said, and by calling my ideas "wise" he shut me up. Age
21, my father thought what *his* father thought

was ridiculous, and railroaded here
to find another Michigan where he was sure silence had
the last word. Where he and his son could sit in darkness
swapping silences until between us we produced a third and final
silence big enough to house the wild inhabitants and keep alive
the kingdom of a sunken island we could swim to, should it rise.

The Vital Statistic

That morning a young man came to nothing on the old linoleum
and each prayer fell harder than the last into alarm.
That evening I shot the survivors with a zoom lens,
their faces went white like pages of a secret diary left open.
People said the usual "he shouldn't have..."
and all at once we began to remember him as a stick figure:
when the suicide had worn off completely he seemed to become, again,
a young man sitting in silence near the chinaberry
or a young man with strong pulse approaching on the run—
but at a hundred yards we could actually see his heartbeat
was a jiggling rhythm of the faultless .45 slug in his breastpocket.
Running by us toward the country of his birth in wild disbelief
he shouted, "I forgot to write a thousand poems about the sea!"

Last Message

Sunrise, I am too many years old.
The reality angel, puzzled and woozy behind the mask
of my unshaven face, glares from the mirror as if remembering
better days when he was only a dark code hidden in my DNA.
I open my eyes slowly, hoping the man I should have been
hit town while I was sleeping and, as if by magic,
disappeared into my body, camoflauged by my deadpan.
But with a sudden wave of my hand I am still here.

Only a few poems after I was born
but already I am lost amid the pines of airwick,
shaving shadows off my face with the silver blade I love
because the name is feminine, almost French, *Gillette*.
Later, I'll escape this one-room studio and climb the iron stairs
where I'll sit and leer at the marquee of the Rialto theater,
a cardboard girl in low-cut chiffon who lounges beneath
the word *Wow*, a double-feature: *Love Thy Neighbors*
and *Let All The Beautiful Be Equal*.

Why didn't I invent the better mousetrap?
Why does all I say sound so forgettable? Egg and sperm,
please help us all: engulfed by a substantial fog two lovers
humped until my character came in waves, somewhere between
genesis and id and oz, a biochemical wash. I try to be
myself. But soon I will descend the iron stairs and try again
to be someone else: the hero of this poem

who sees his sadness in the dark
displays of secondhand shops and dreamy boutiques
when he walks home at five o'clock, the lights going out.
Sometimes, I feel hidden by all this, a stowaway.
Sometimes, arrested by faces in the foggy glass,

I am stopped by what appears to be real emotion
playing on the faces of mannequins, angels of dismay.
It is as if I saw their thoughts and they saw a small
spirit on the street, who is only me of course, oh
nobody special on a white horse.

I, Said the Donkey

So I failed my audition
for eternal star and fell on all fours in the shadows
with my classmates, a musically-gifted farm animal.
We sang about the burdens and joys of being Jesus
while the holy family ducked the curtain coming down
and smells of Dentyne and liquor rose from the yawning
audience, a clear sign this illusion was finished
for another year. In the darkness backstage

I imagined Jesus on his flight
through the roof into heaven, rising on the static
of television airwaves, dodging episodes of *Guiding Light*.
I stood in awe for a moment, in my donkey suit, and
recalled the whole story like an old soap: child-star
wooed by three talent scouts, the big Bethlehem debut,
Judas and the fatal kiss, a ruined career he toasted
with a final drink of vinegar and brief comeback,
the sky opening and closing.

The angels who got such good reviews
still make a cameo appearance year after year
but they've suffered major alterations in character
and fly in circles on the parlor table like dancers
shackled to a small carousel. They carry spears
and make monotonous music on golden shells until
the candles burn down and I stop them, still hot,
as if they've flown here from hell.

Someday, I shall be an angel myself:
patron saint of the lost Rockettes, patron saint
of the peaceful countenance of ducks in an arcade.
On Xmas, I'll drink just enough to leave one half-inch

of wine in the glass, my application for a second
chance from anyone who knows God. I will walk uptown
in my old boots. I will wear the white beard and bash
the brass bell, heckle passing strangers

for pennies and more pennies
to help me save the world. I will speak outloud
new versions of old prayers that went unanswered
last year. I will sing the hymns. And I will sweat.
Saving a world is hard work. Looking into the window
of Rexall Drugs I will see the small nativity:
some lazy cows, three handsome Kings, poor Joseph
and the babe in cellophane, the startled virgin.

All About Love

One 30-watt bulb is my weak link between
now and dawn. In hundreds of rooms like my own
hundreds of men and women sleep with men and women
and the smell of sex is dark and strong, sardines.
Someone who must be lonely makes a loud catcall,
stone lion lost in reverie on steps of the asylum.
The only light that burns all night in this city
is mine, a 30-watt bulb with no hidden meaning
but my own. The city is dark, as if sleepers
share a secret and must flee into the same dream
tomorrow will bring a yesterday worth something.

In Winter

I can't see Father Time from here, but I can see his zodiac
and black moustache. Sitting in my room on Summit Avenue
I see myself, false starts, small steps, in shorthand
tics of the clock. I am time's sluggish scout. I am
whoever I said I was in the last message written
by my venus pencil in the margins of this poem.
Seconds pulse against my bony wrist. Whole moments pass.
Lives I thought I loved the most have all escaped, like crows
that circle in my subconscious, each a small black x in flight.

I am only one of many hundred Johns on this planet, at any rate,
I am here on special assignment, code-name *now:* Shoo death off.
I shoo death off until the crows fly back with no good news
about the hostage, Father Time. That no two snowflakes are alike
reminds me of the fact that single clues might come from any one
of many hundred clocks. But all the clock will say is *tsk, tsk, tsk.*
My thoughts have all escaped the way that frenzied crows escape
the sky by flying into snow, in winter, into the slow brainmeat.

Poem With Nothing to Say

The moon is half-hidden by the eyelid of one cloud
and I sit by the bed. The girl sleeps, but if she wakes
I must know what to say, questions which aren't questions,
a difficult test in which her answers can't be false or true:
I have no fear of water. I have no fear of fire. I never dream.
I loved my mother. I loved my father. I have few or no pains.
The doctors have gone home to dreams of curing the common cold
and I sit by the bed composing a poem in my head about drugs
whose names remind me of gods in ancient Rome, Haldol and Prolixin.
Along one wall are large books about the unknown which offer
no help at all: beyond the plexiglass shield there are twenty

rooms where warm bodies sleep off the effects of cold fact.
The staff sit in the staff-room discussing phases of the moon
but I sit by the bed. *There is something wrong with my mind.*
Often I cross the street to avoid people who can read my thoughts.
Often I feel unreal. I sweat easily even on the coolest days.
I am a special agent of God. I would like to be a singer.
There is nothing in this world to be afraid of, I once said.
The girl sleeps, but if she wakes she'll do something grand:
upend the nightstand and thrash from bed as if she wrestles
a dragon, knowing what to say cannot be said, biting her hand.

Poem With Sedative Effect

On the hospital unit where I work
a young girl wrote "I love you" on the walls

with excrement. A valentine of shit.
I wrote in the proper blank space, "Patient

has apparently expressed hard feelings
on the evening of the 25th." There are

no easy feelings in the books I've read
about the schizophrenic, psychopath,

psychotic. "There are feelings lodged between
my stomach and my mouth I can't cough up,"

she said. Then she wept because
the color of some old hallway linoleum

was very red. I knew
of no technical term for such an act, I wrote

"This patient does not seem to be herself."
I meant neither one of us knew who she was.

Pleased to be involved in the act of love
anyone could issue

the ugly, guttural noises she did.
She called every name of god

from Lucky Stars to Elohim.
Thorazine finally put her to sleep.

Because I am instructed to mistrust appearances
every fifteen minutes

I was an astronaut lost in space
and charted the position of the girl who never moved.

She was like a mural of the dark and stars.
In a blank space on the brainboard I wrote

"Patient has apparently slept last night."
And then I went home and wrote this poem at dawn.

One Minute of Night Sky

I worked for a year in the cellar
of an airtight clinic, trudged through a valley of cabinets
in a gray smock. My job was filing bulging folders of the dead:
I carried a wire basket through the alphabet, dumping envelopes
of aneurism, cancer and cerebral lesion into yawning racks.
I could travel decades in a few steps,

   stop and page through a chart until
I was in the blue hills west of brain damage, dwindling hills
and rivers of red that met in flatlands on a black horizon,
ticker-tape from the electroencephalograph. Stapled on last
reports of death there was a small snapshot from the morgue,
a face no larger than my thumbprint.

   The work made me sick.
Reading histories of tumors and fatal transplants
until the lines on graphs convulsed and snarled like wiring
come loose in a circuit for the mind of God. Once, I saw
close-ups of the malignancy which killed a man my age,
nothing much on the x-ray,

   a blemish vague as memory,
a burr which swam through nervous systems into his brain.
I could have sworn he was staring back at me from his worn
snapshot but, of course, he wasn't. He couldn't. His eyes
were shut. I put him away with unusual force and heard
his chart jar the rack, as if something

   small had gone off, a mousetrap.
The next day I quit. For the first night in weeks, I slept.
But in my deepest sleep, even now, if the chemicals balance
and tissues are ripe, a synapse forms the memory: iron
spring slips, the trap shuts, my eyes fly open and all
the darkness around me wakes.

Supposedly, each human being
has a built-in-mechanism for one minute of knowing
he or she will someday die. One minute of night sky: life
going on across the street where someone greets darkness
with tins of food and drink, where someone listens, pauses
by the door and throws the bolt and lets the animal in.

Keeping Still, Mountain

Looking through ads for drill-press
operators, caretakers, inventory analysts, beauticians
and warehouse helpers, I remembered what my father said
about Puritan ethics, and my heritage, the American Dream.
Although I've since forgotten what he said I know I spent
hours in a local cafeteria, paging through ads
and throwing I-Ching.

Pennies clattered on the cold formica
as my hexagrams predicted full-time unemployment,
full-time meditation in the cafeteria: smoking cigarettes
and drinking coffee, firm and central in my own immense
fog area. The hexagrams knew all about my job hysteria,
and each hexagram contained some landscape with a missing
person, and a window with an ad for "help wanted."

I remember what my father said
when I told him I'd been advised against pursuing a career
by a book of ancient Chinese wisdom, he was silent.
Keeping still, mountain had advised me to remain detached
from real life, sitting in the local cafeteria and keeping
still, in meditation, smoking cigarettes and drinking coffee,
trying hard to understand the mountain.

It was my father who explained the mountain—
he brought me to a small plot in south Minneapolis, purchased
in the late thirties when real estate was cheap, my grave.
We stood in the mud by my grave. Uphill, near the mausoleum,
drill-press operators, caretakers, inventory analysts, beauticians
and warehouse helpers slumbered under granite and riderless
horses reared back from eternal torches sunk in yellow grass.
My grave was surrounded by white stones like a small crowd
of mourners whose faces had been worn off

by the long wait,
my father said, "If you dare knock the granite statues down
and pile these white stones high, dismantle the mausoleum
and unearth these rock-plaques, it could take you many long years
to work the whole earth bare, and still you'd never understand,
but if you did, the moment you finish, the mountain will be there."

Photo by Nellie DeBruyn

John Engman was born in 1949. He earned degrees from Augsburg College and The University of Iowa Writers' Workshop. In 1977, he received a Minnesota State Arts Board Creative Writing grant, and in 1983, a Loft-McKnight Writers Award. He currently lives in Minneapolis.